Pass the Doodle Art
A coloring book for everyone

Contained within this book are imperfectly drawn lines, circles, squares and many shapes for your coloring enjoyment. Add some color and don't worry about staying in the lines.
Relax and have fun!

Place a scrap piece of paper behind the page you are coloring to prevent bleed-through.

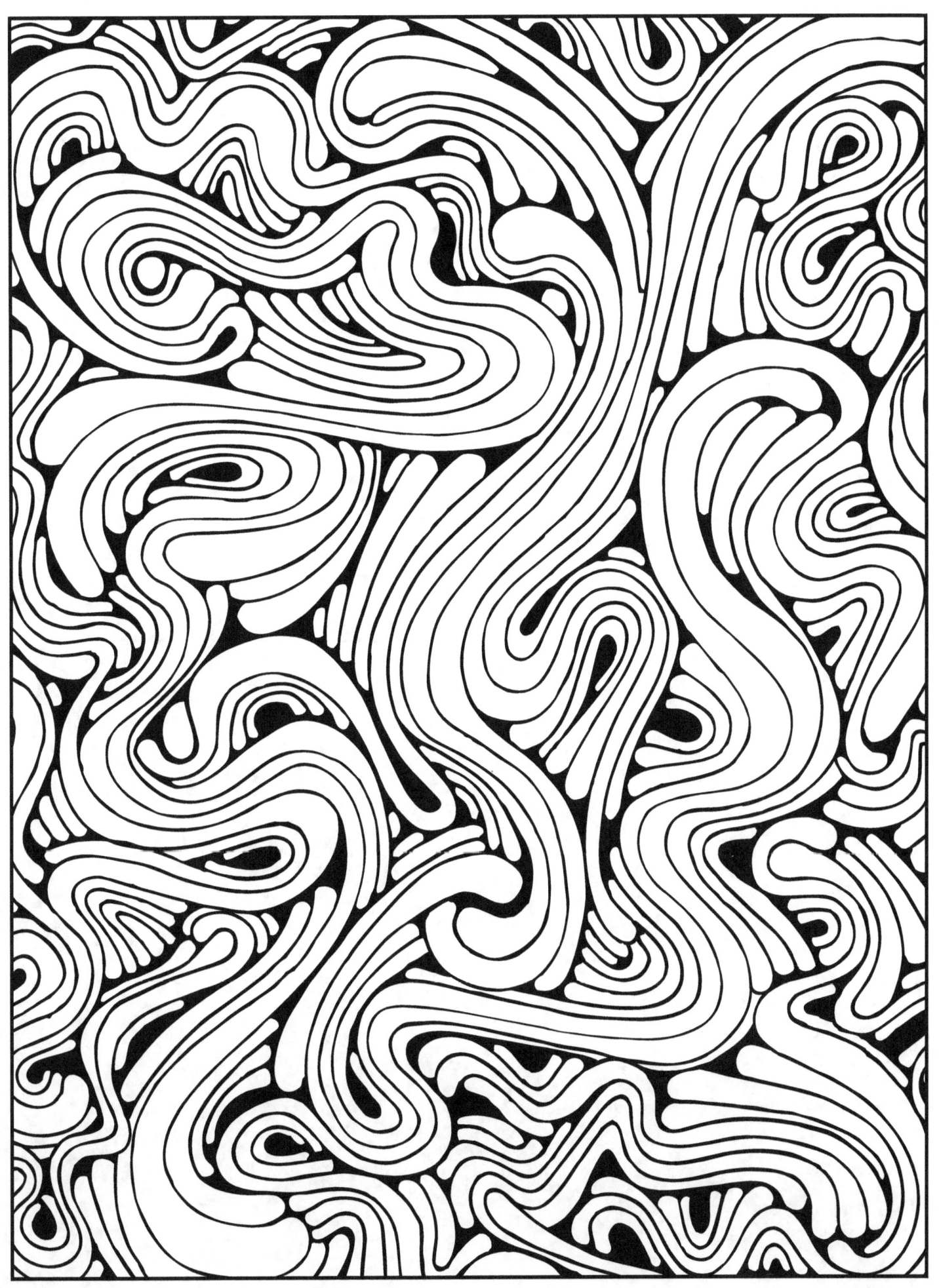

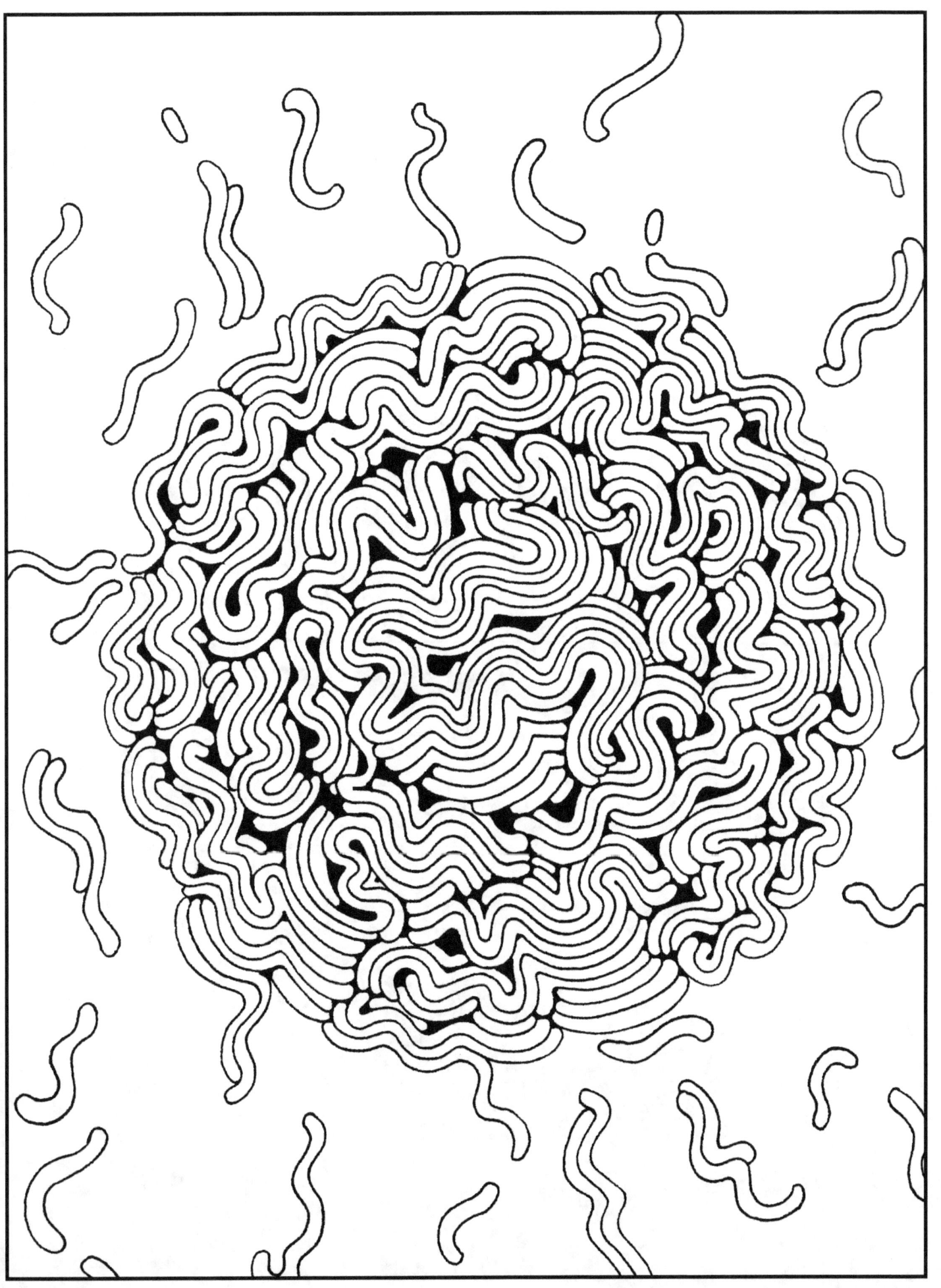

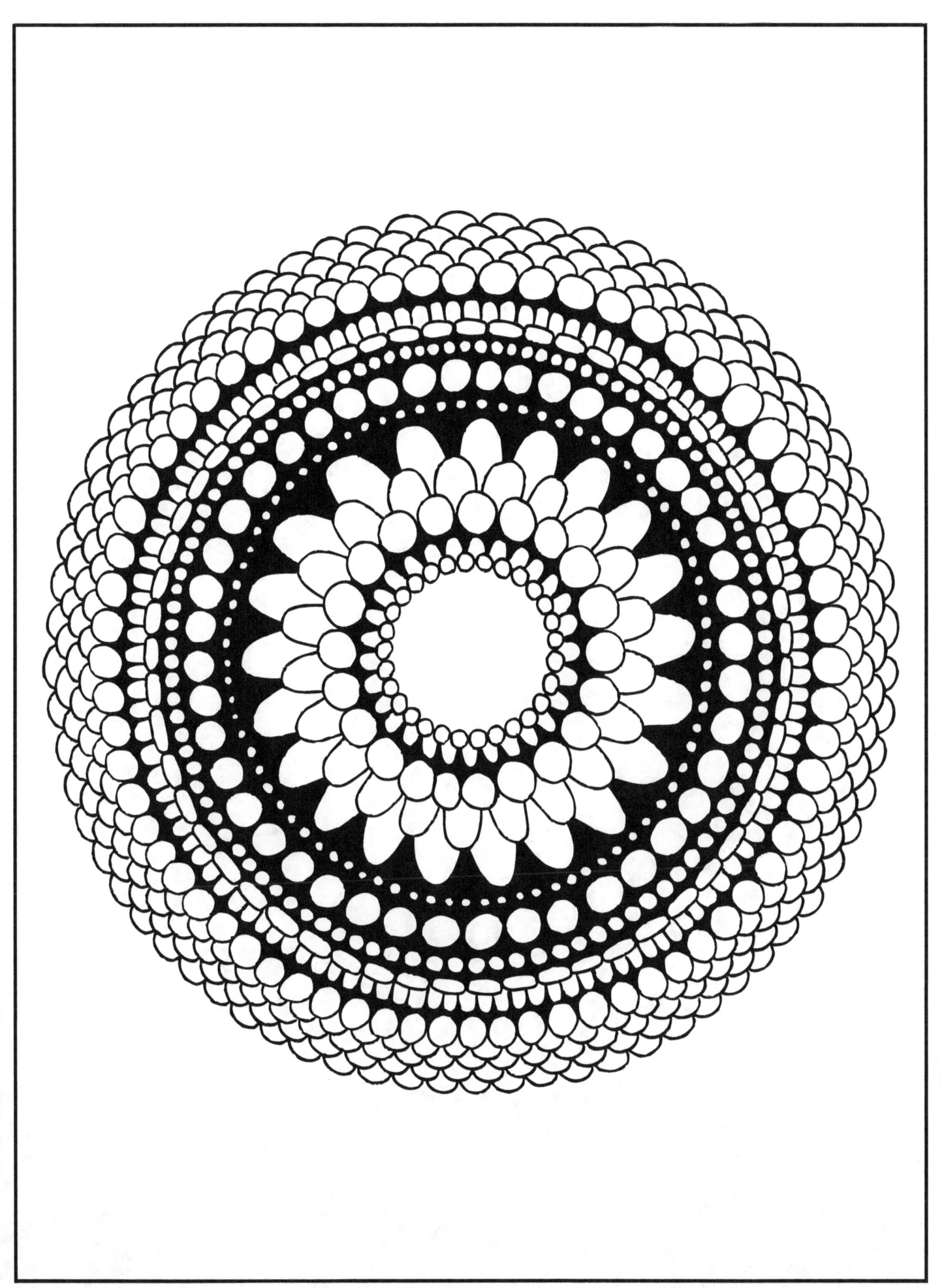

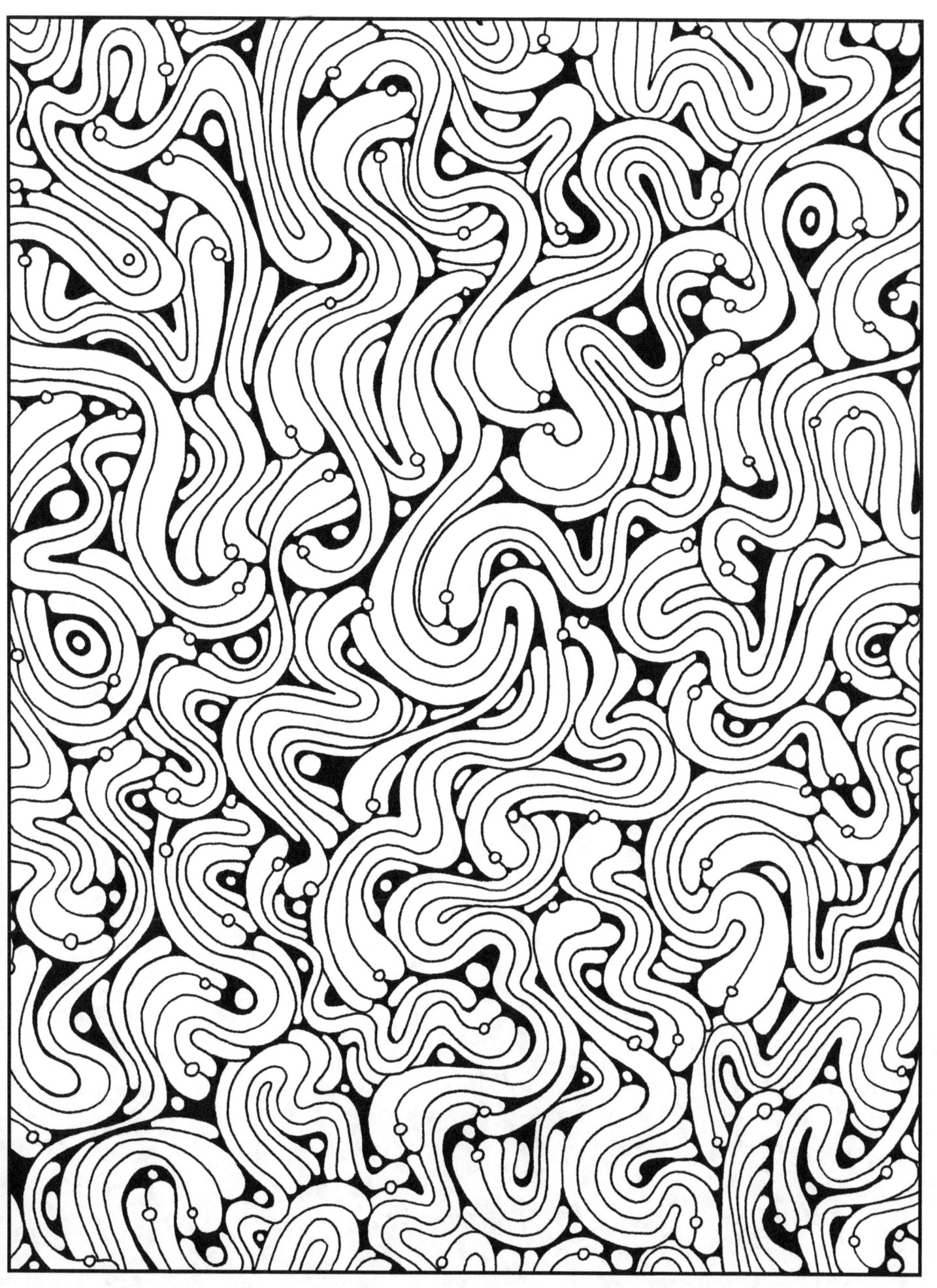

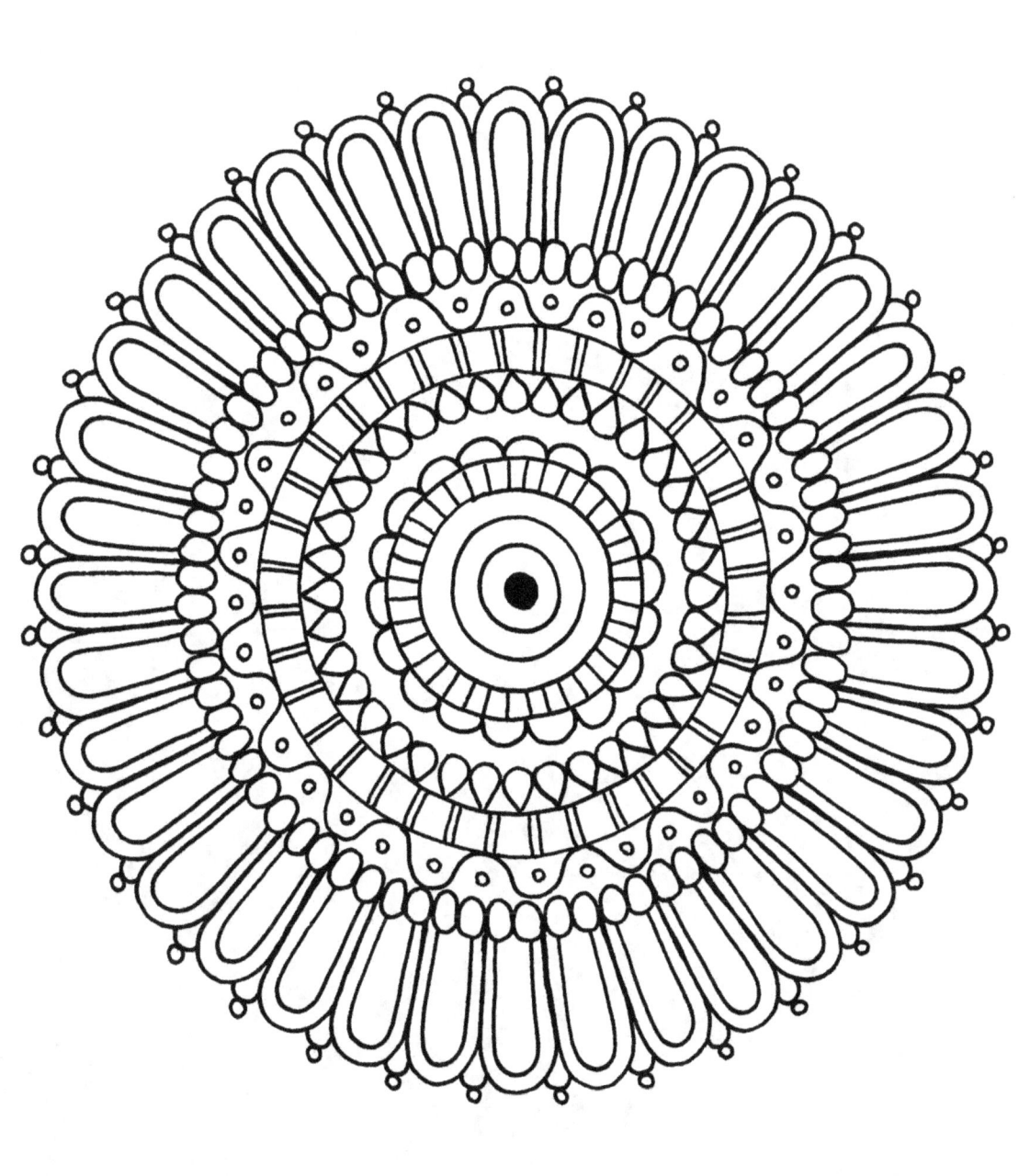

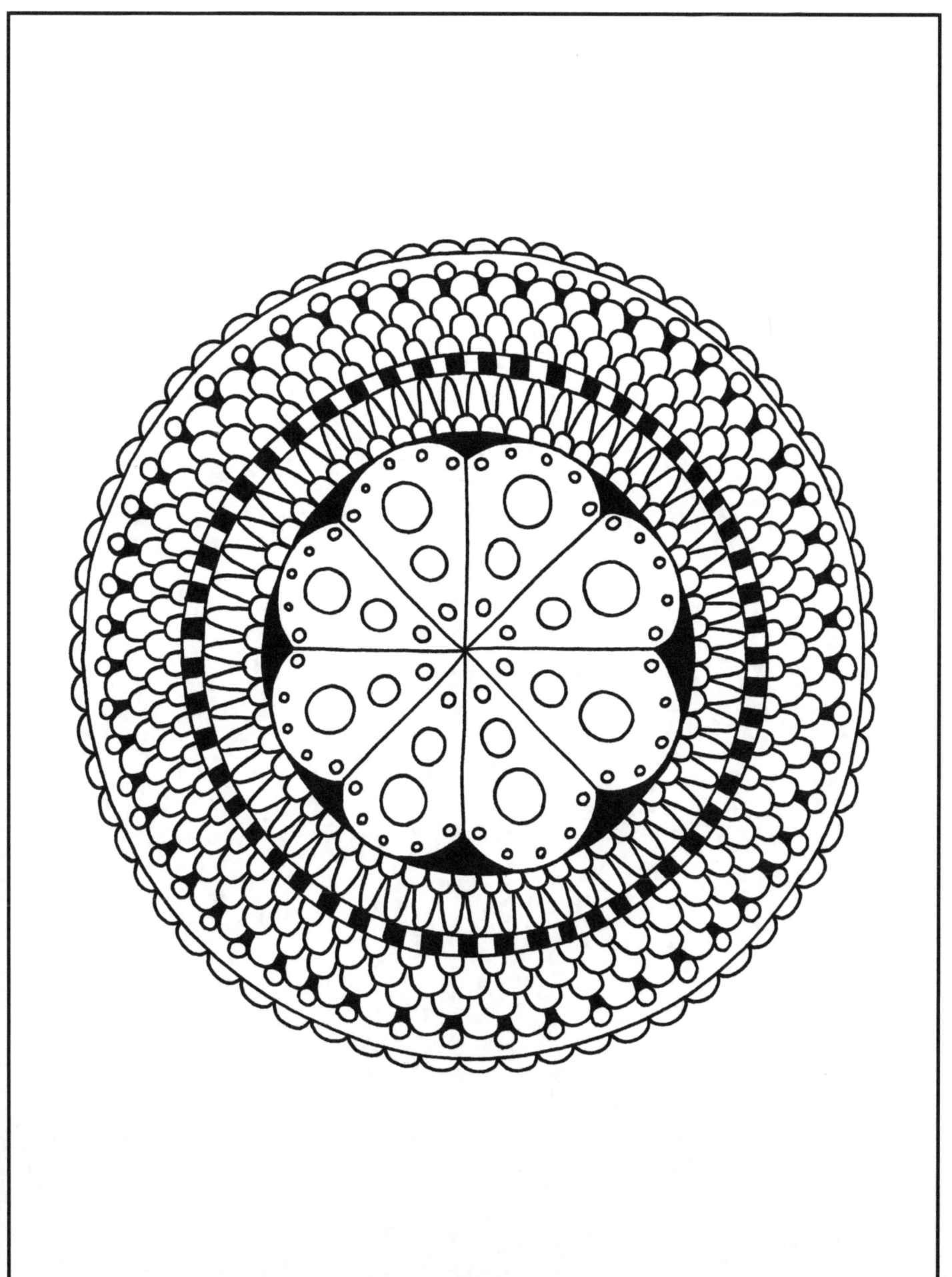

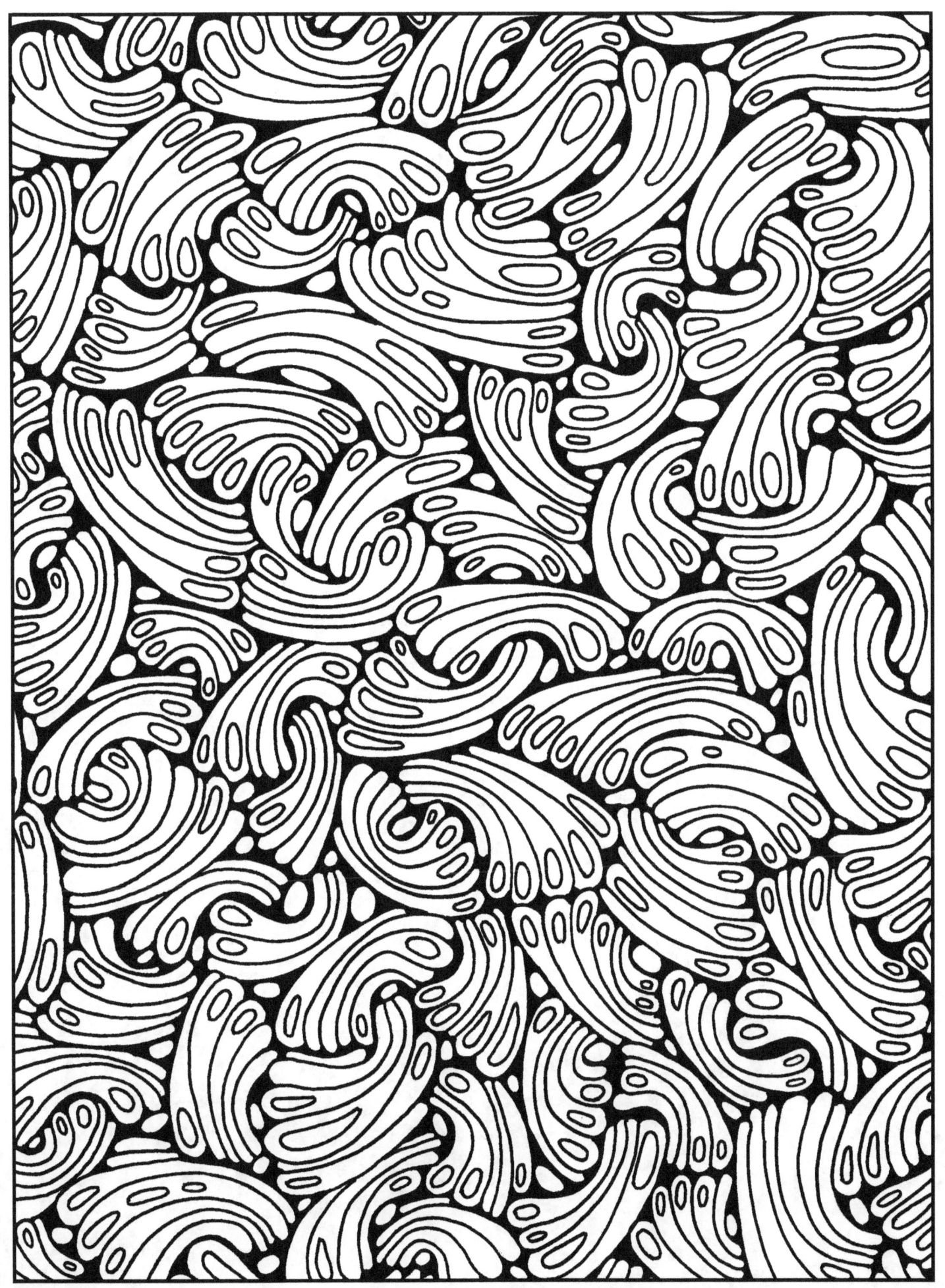

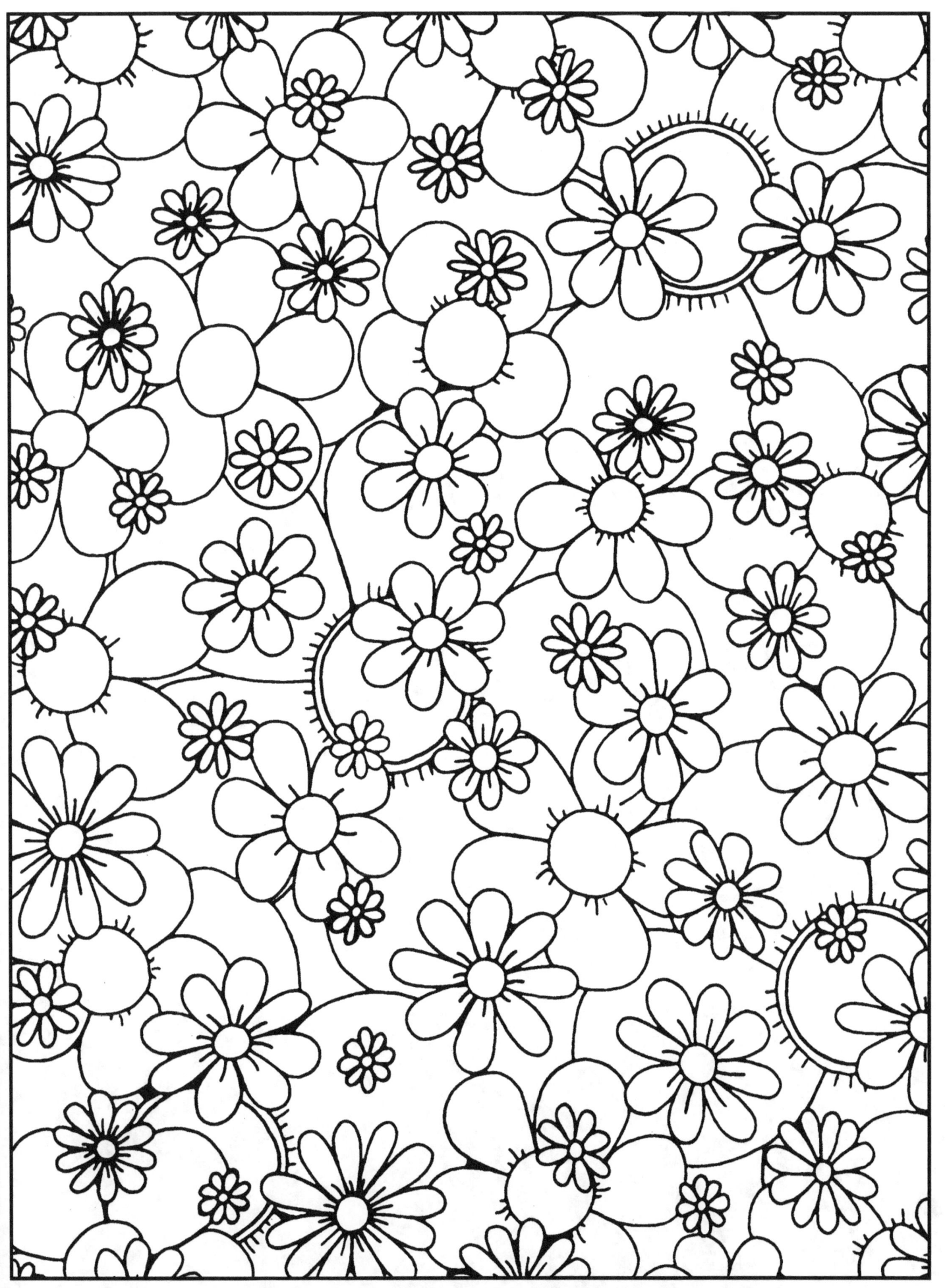

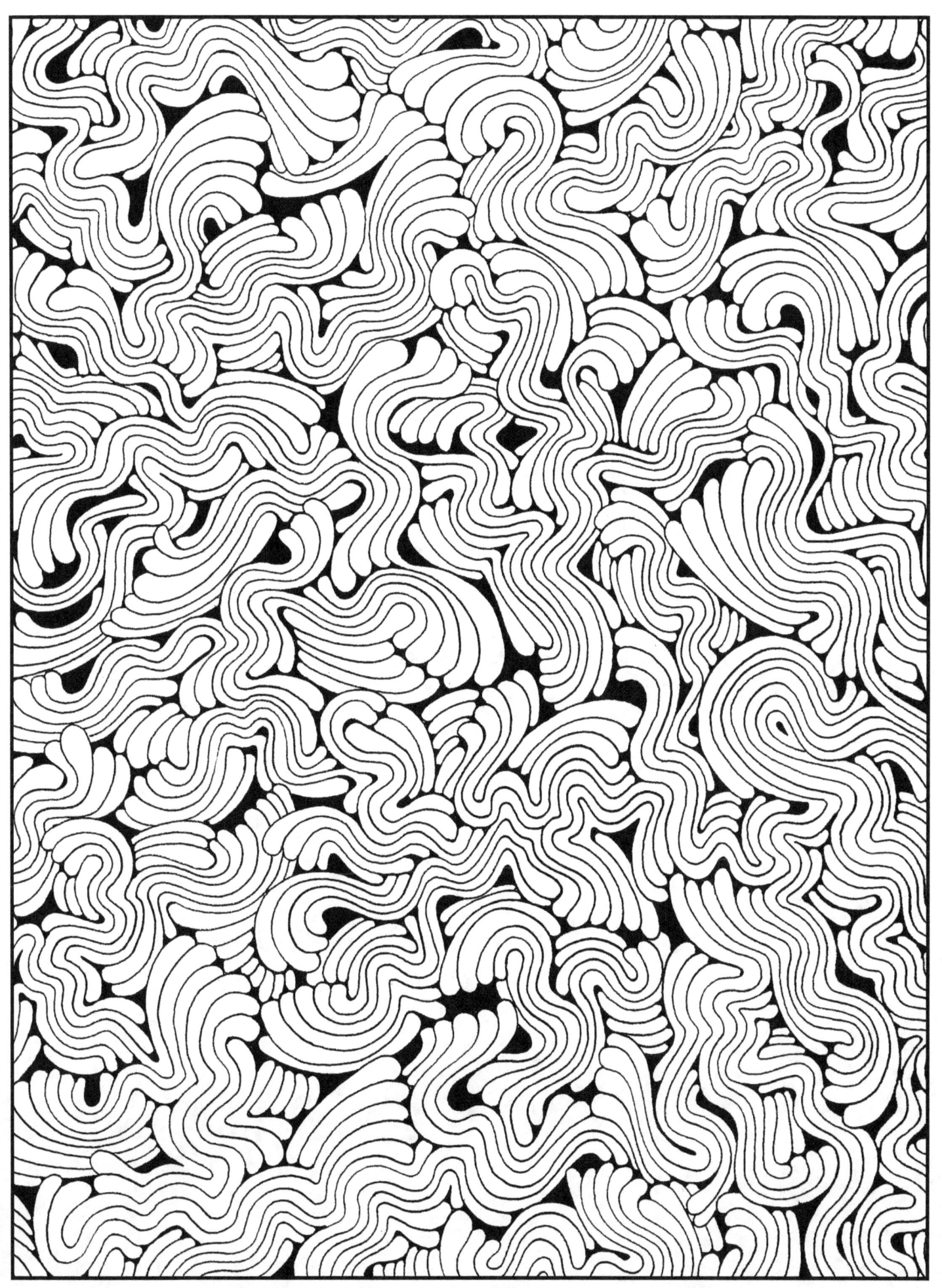

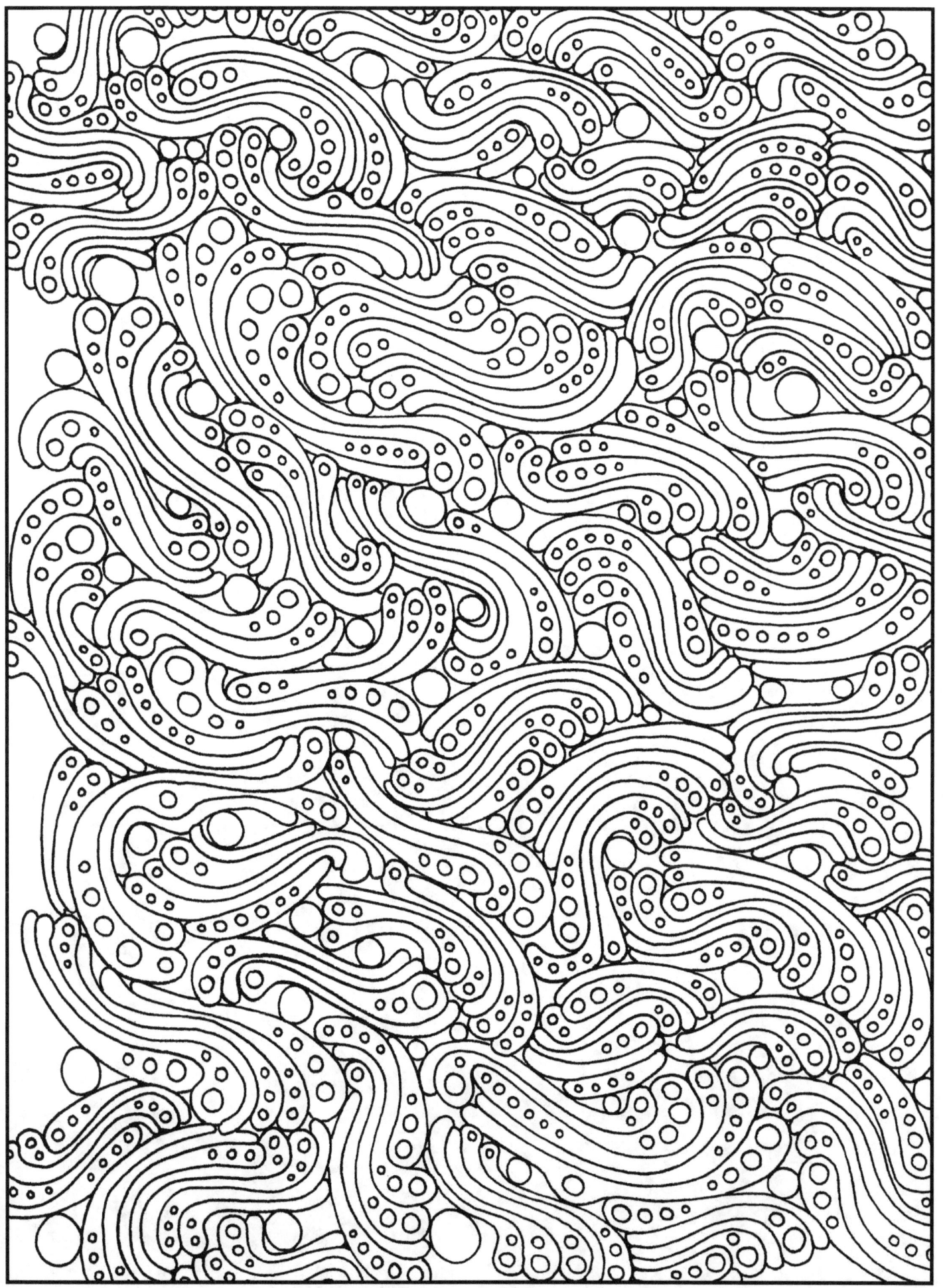

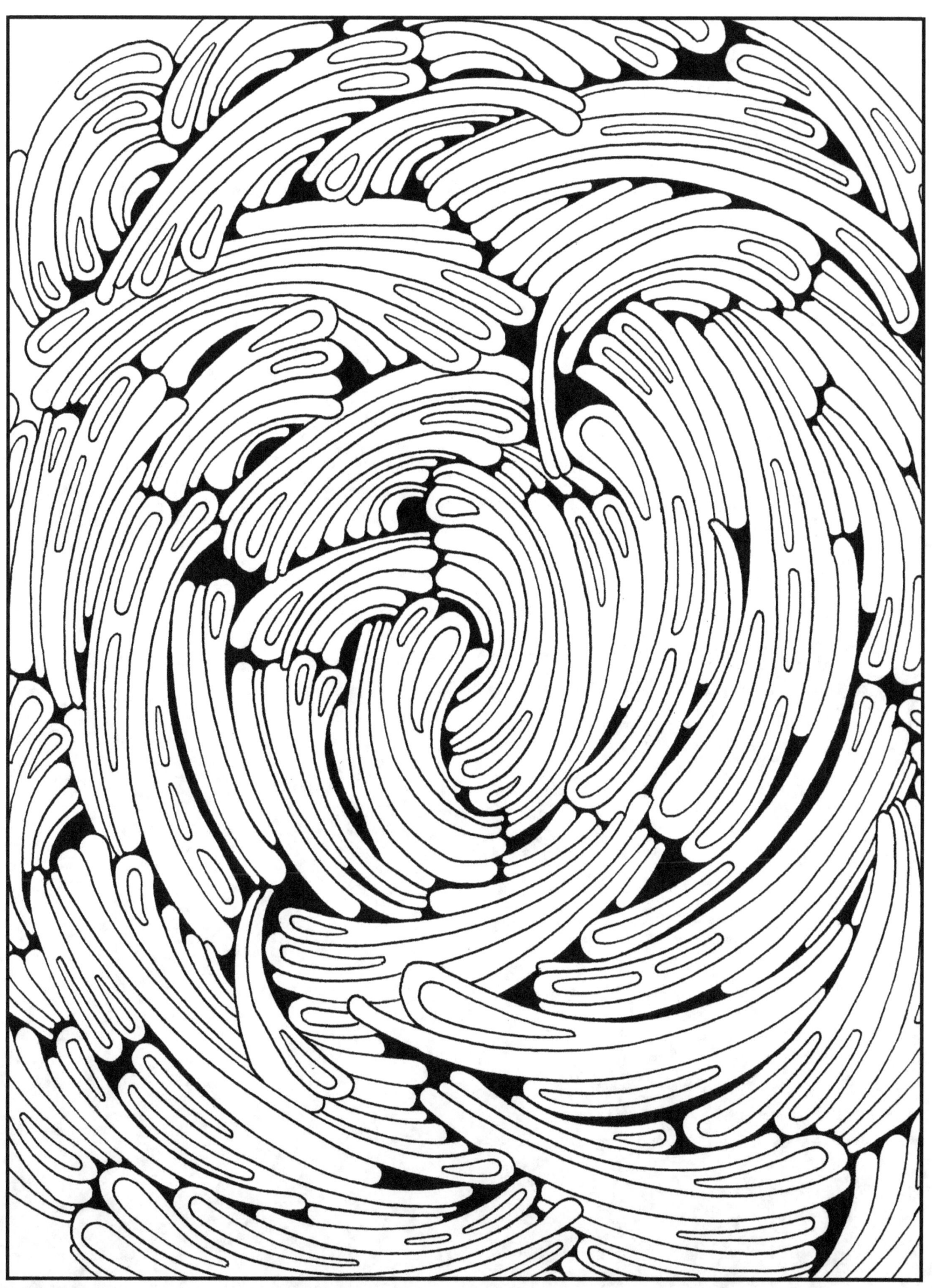

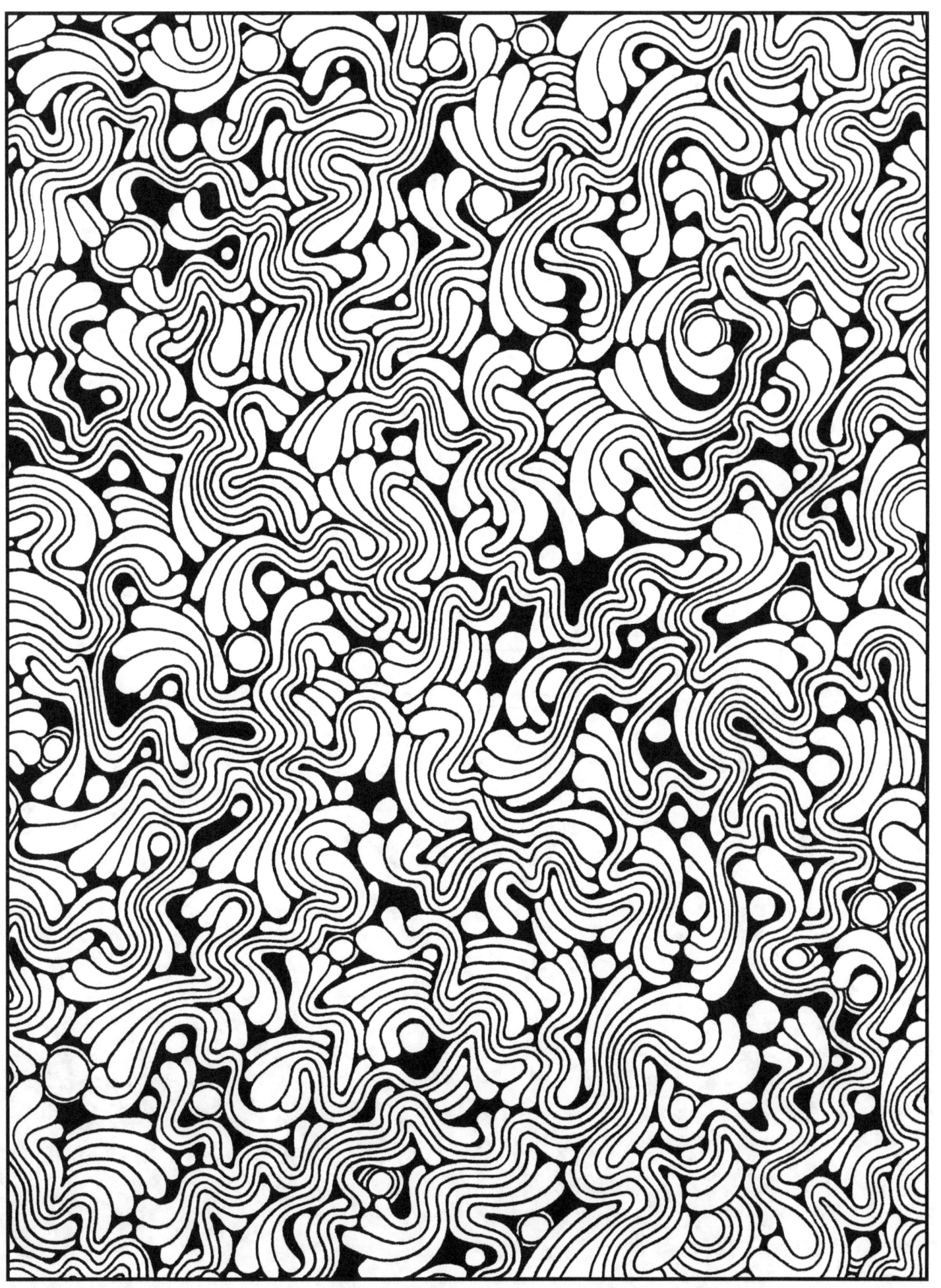

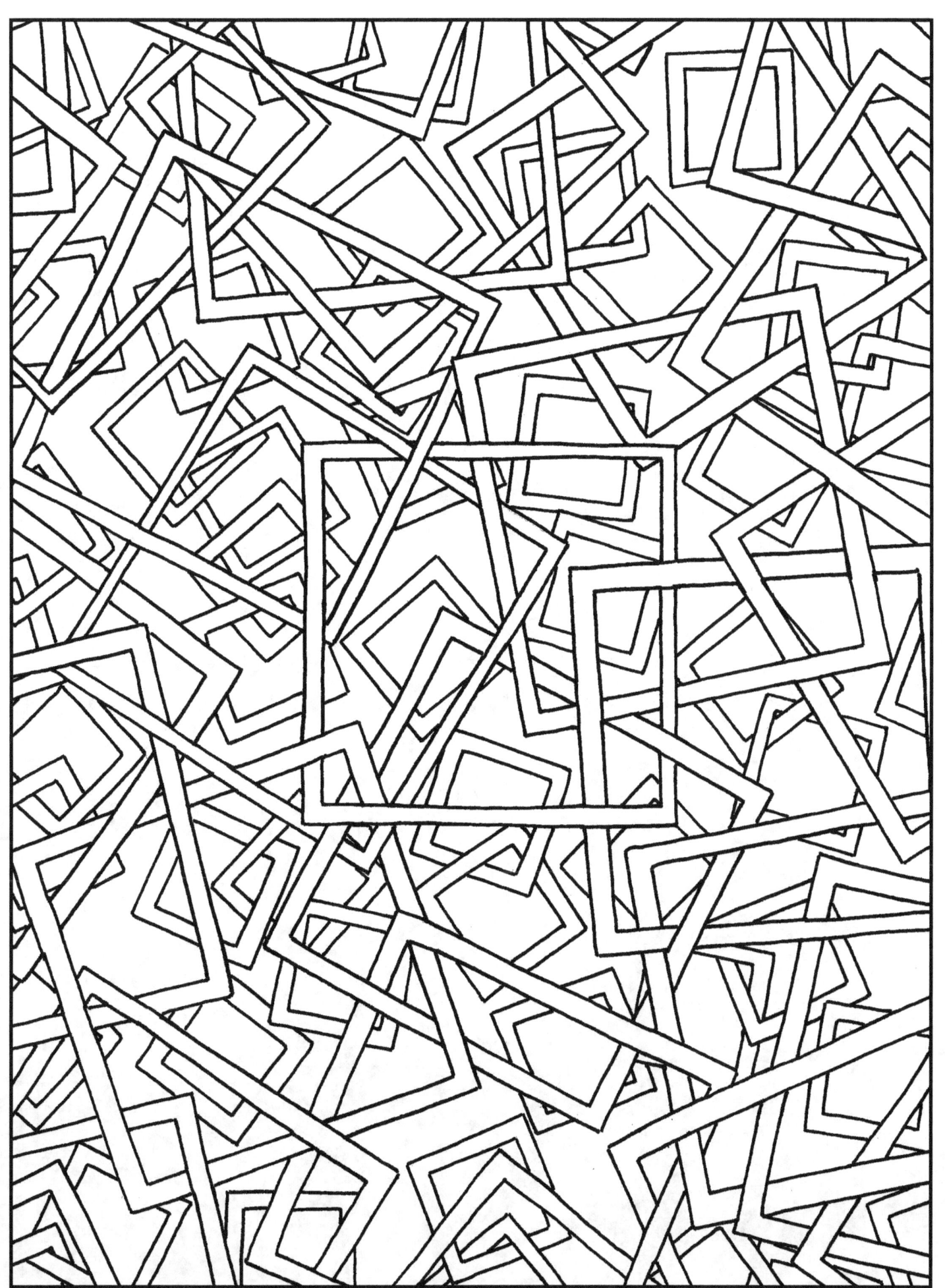

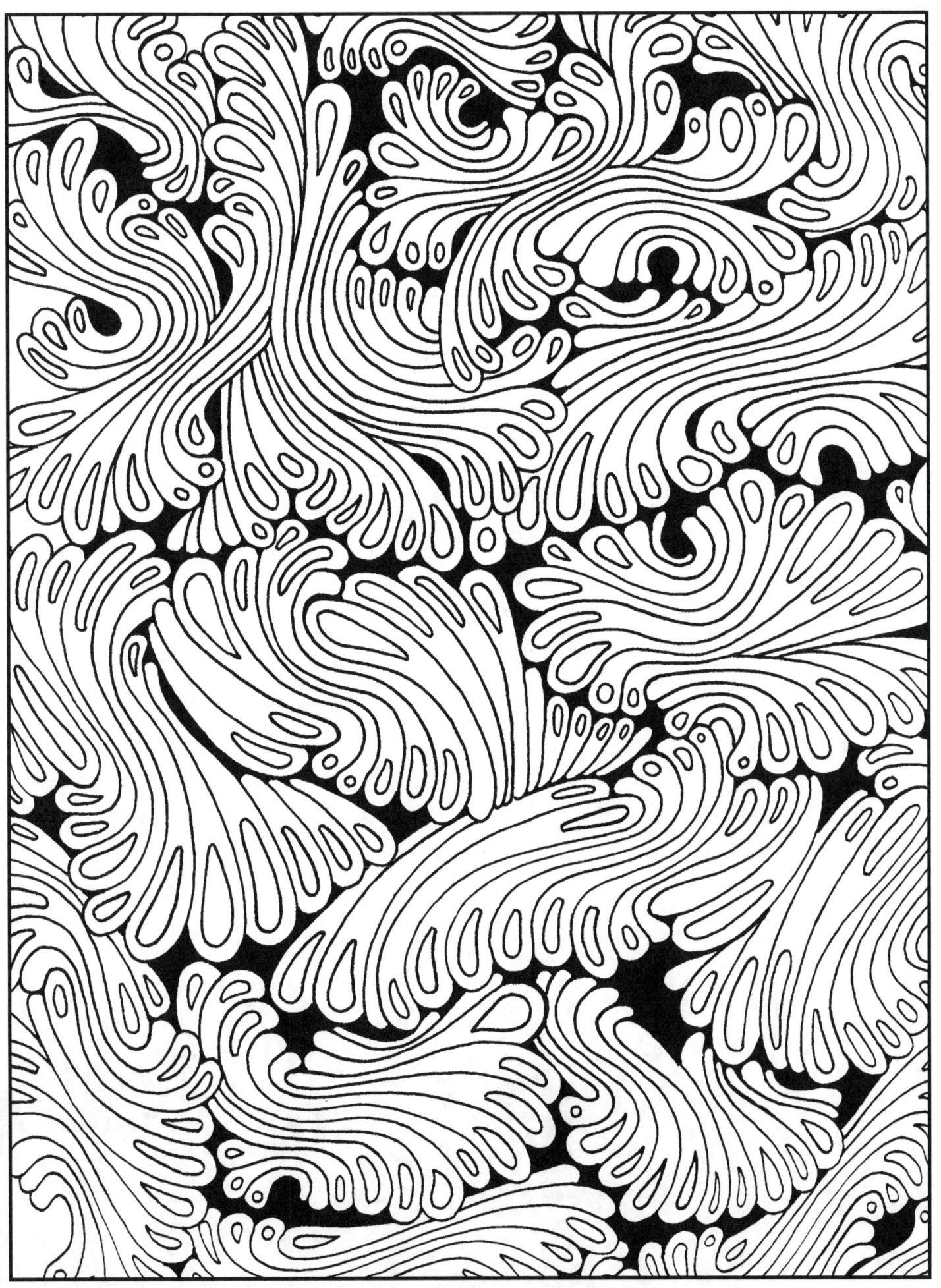

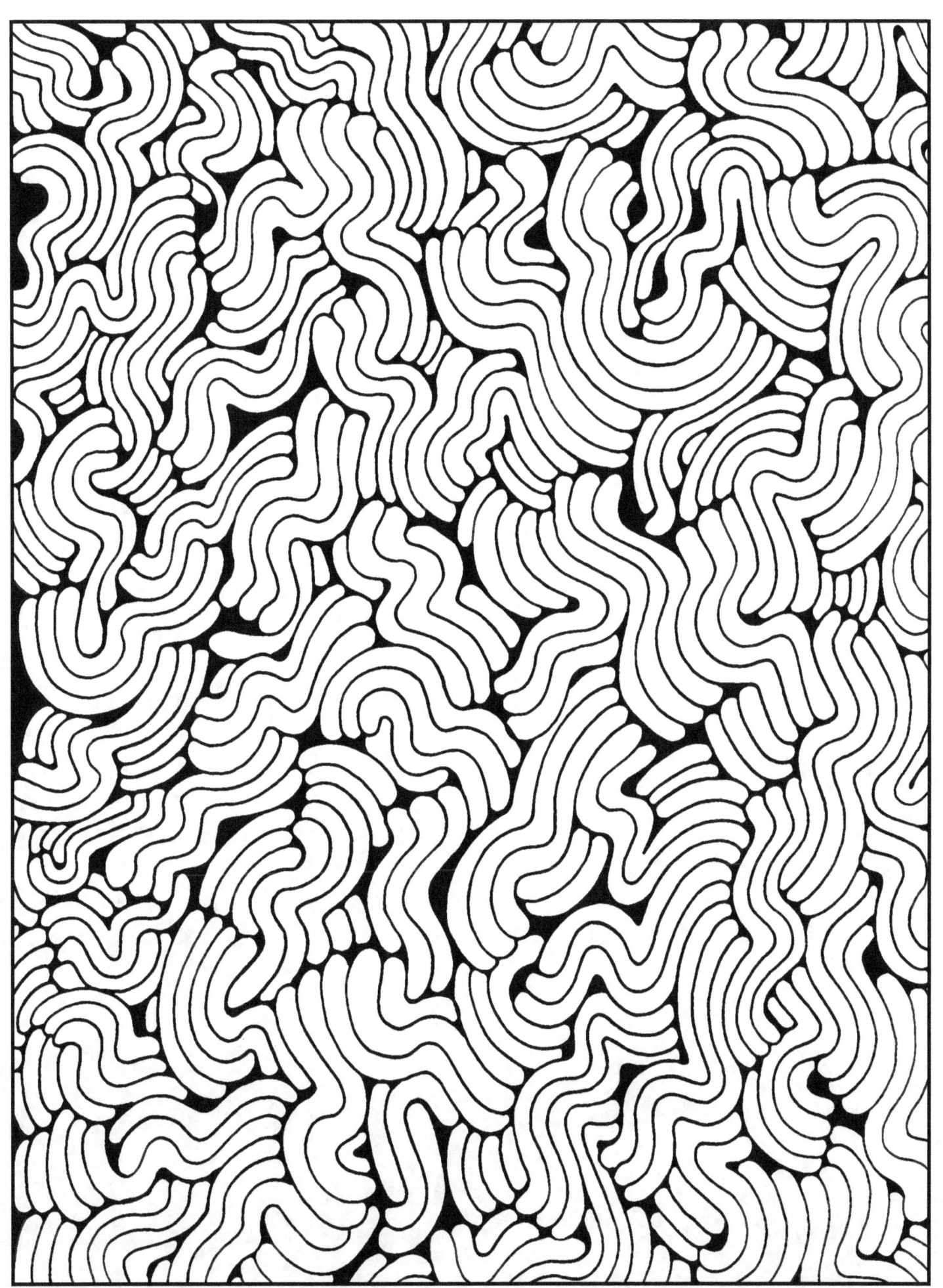

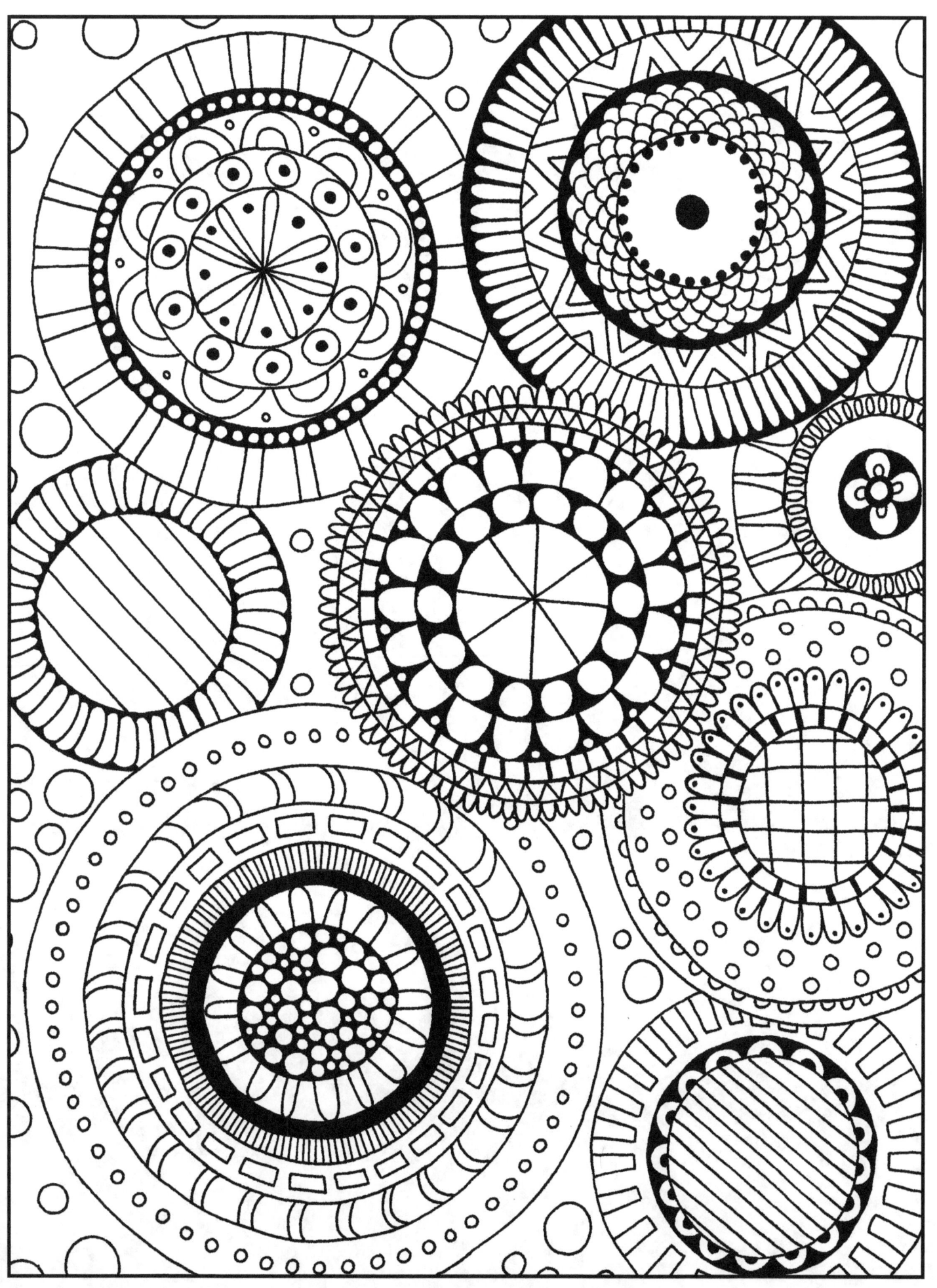

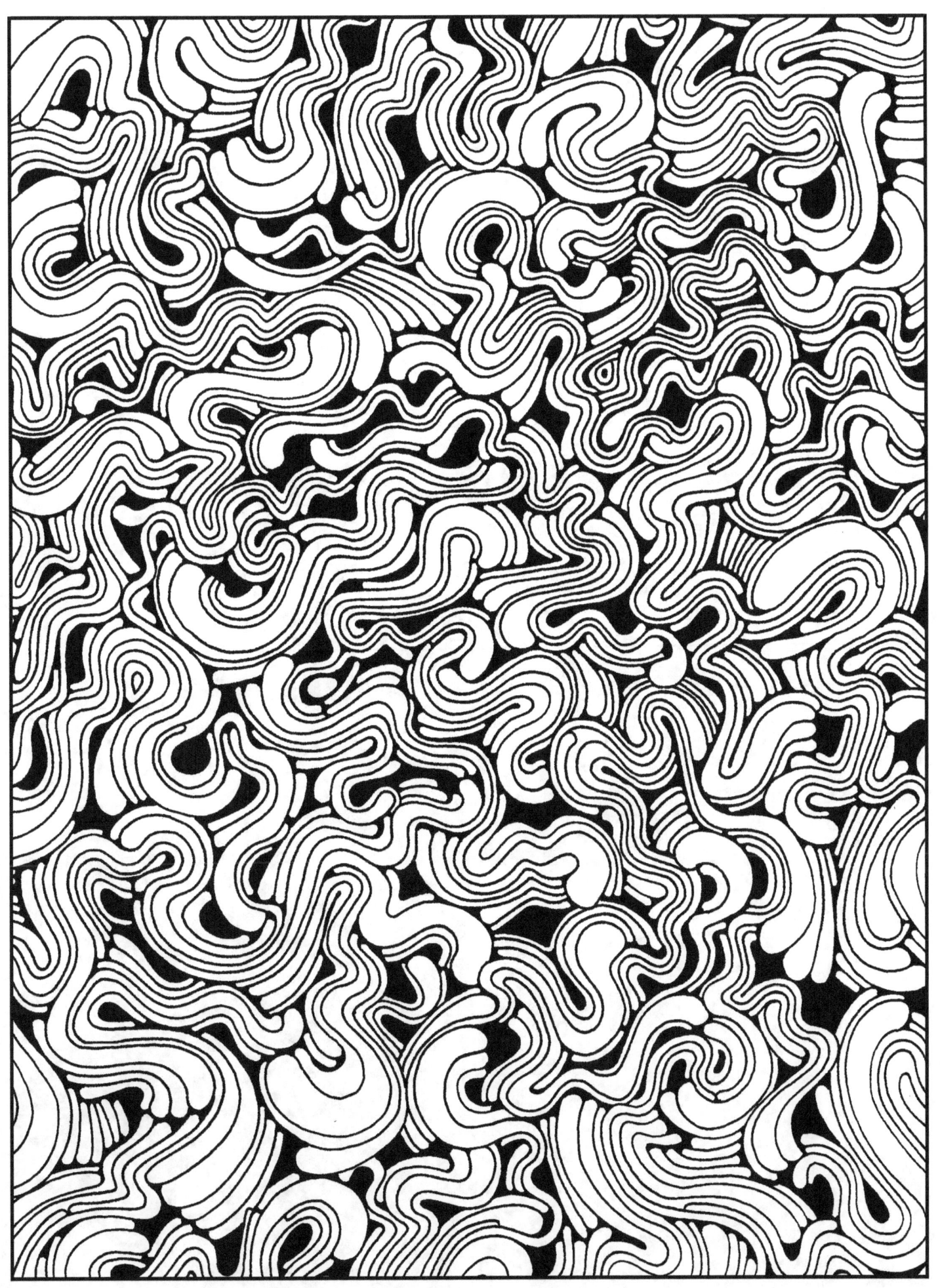

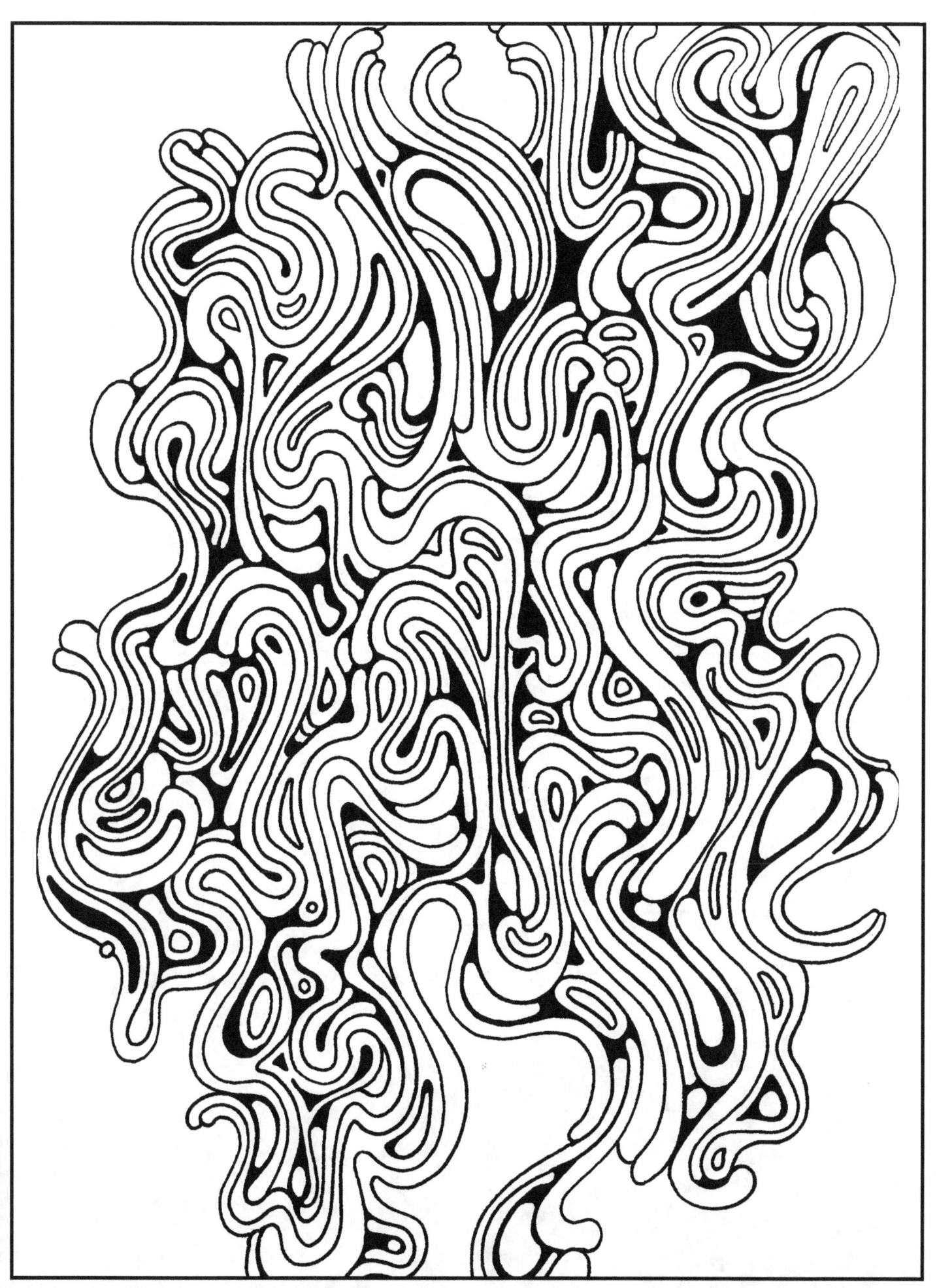

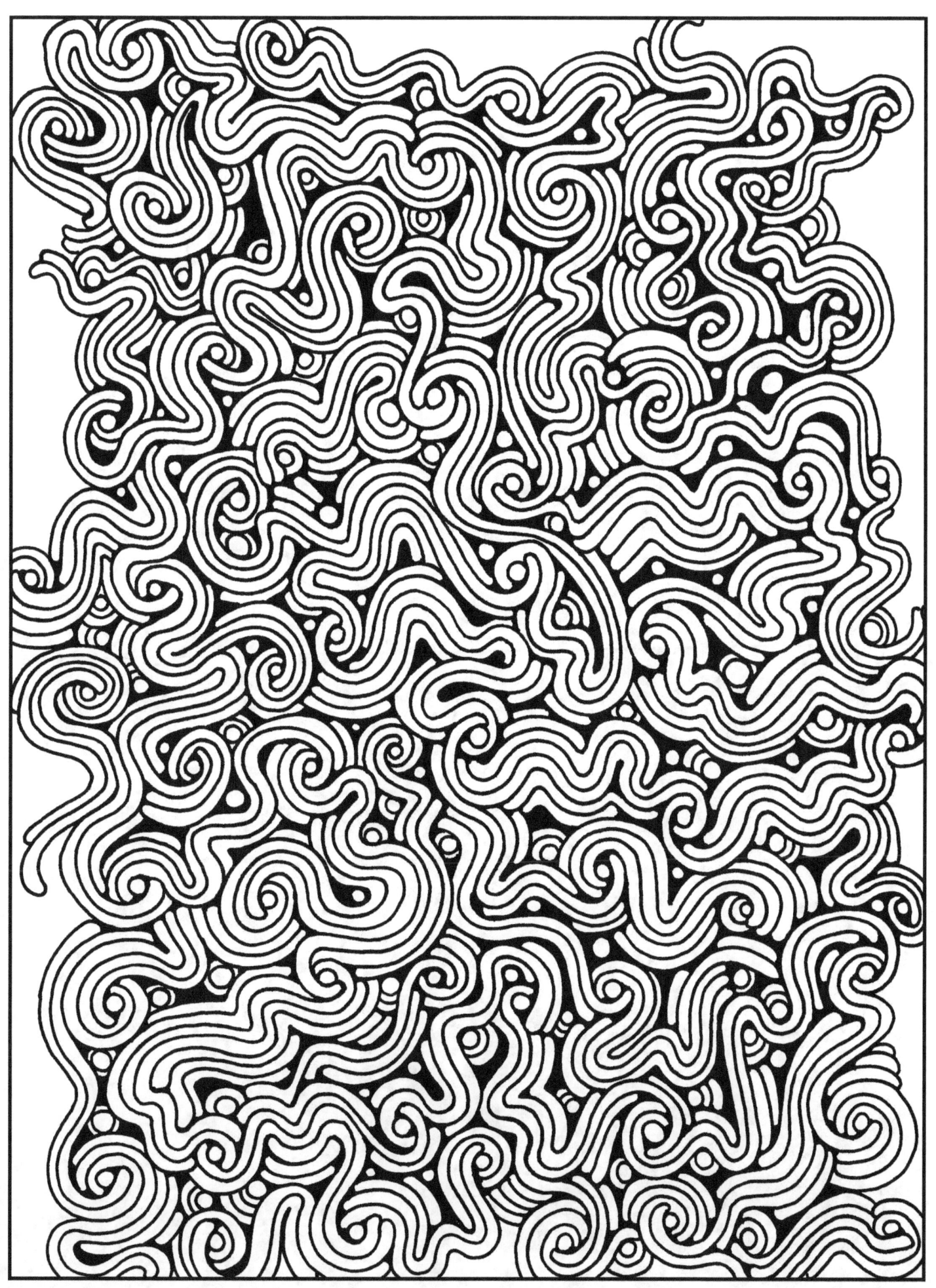

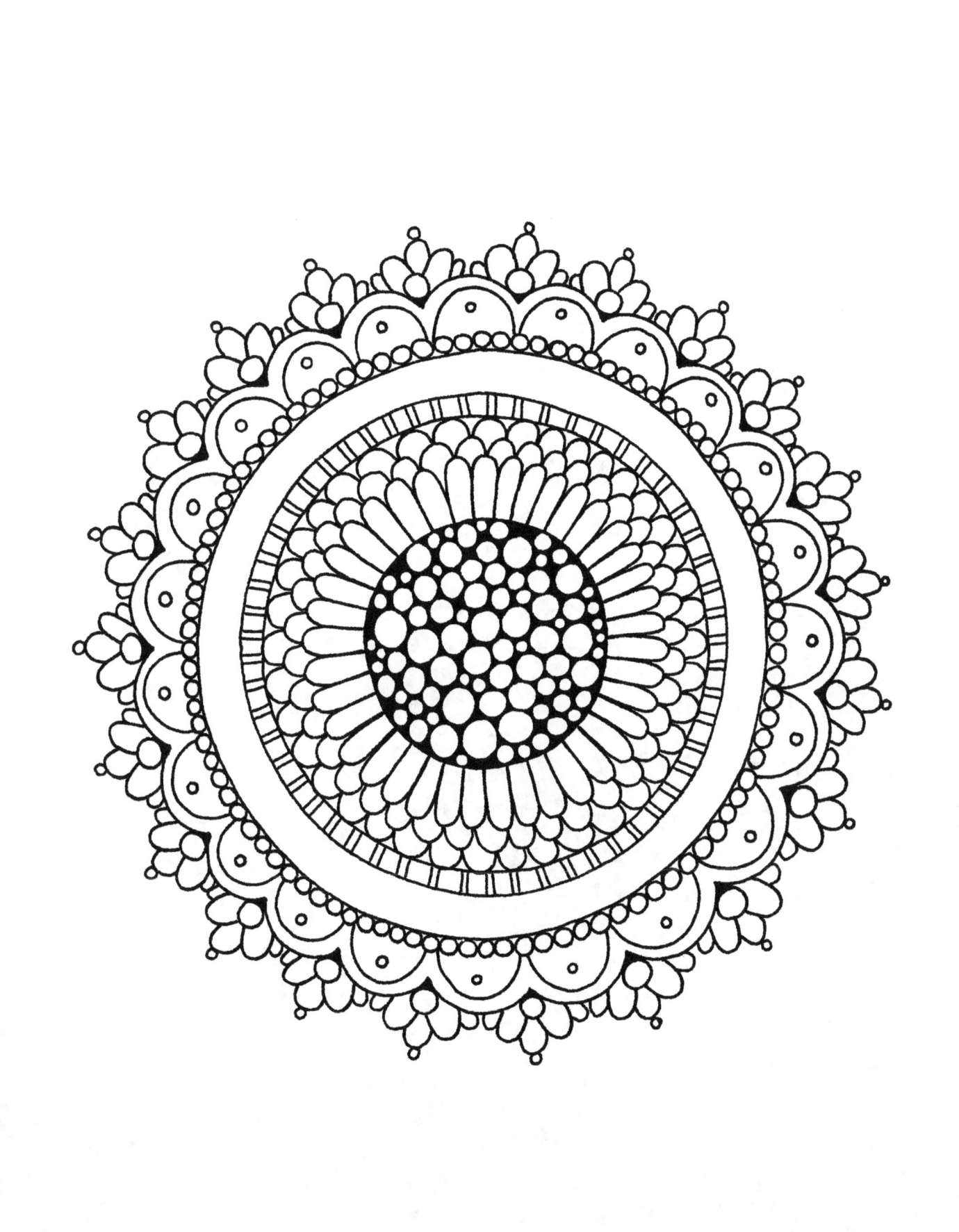

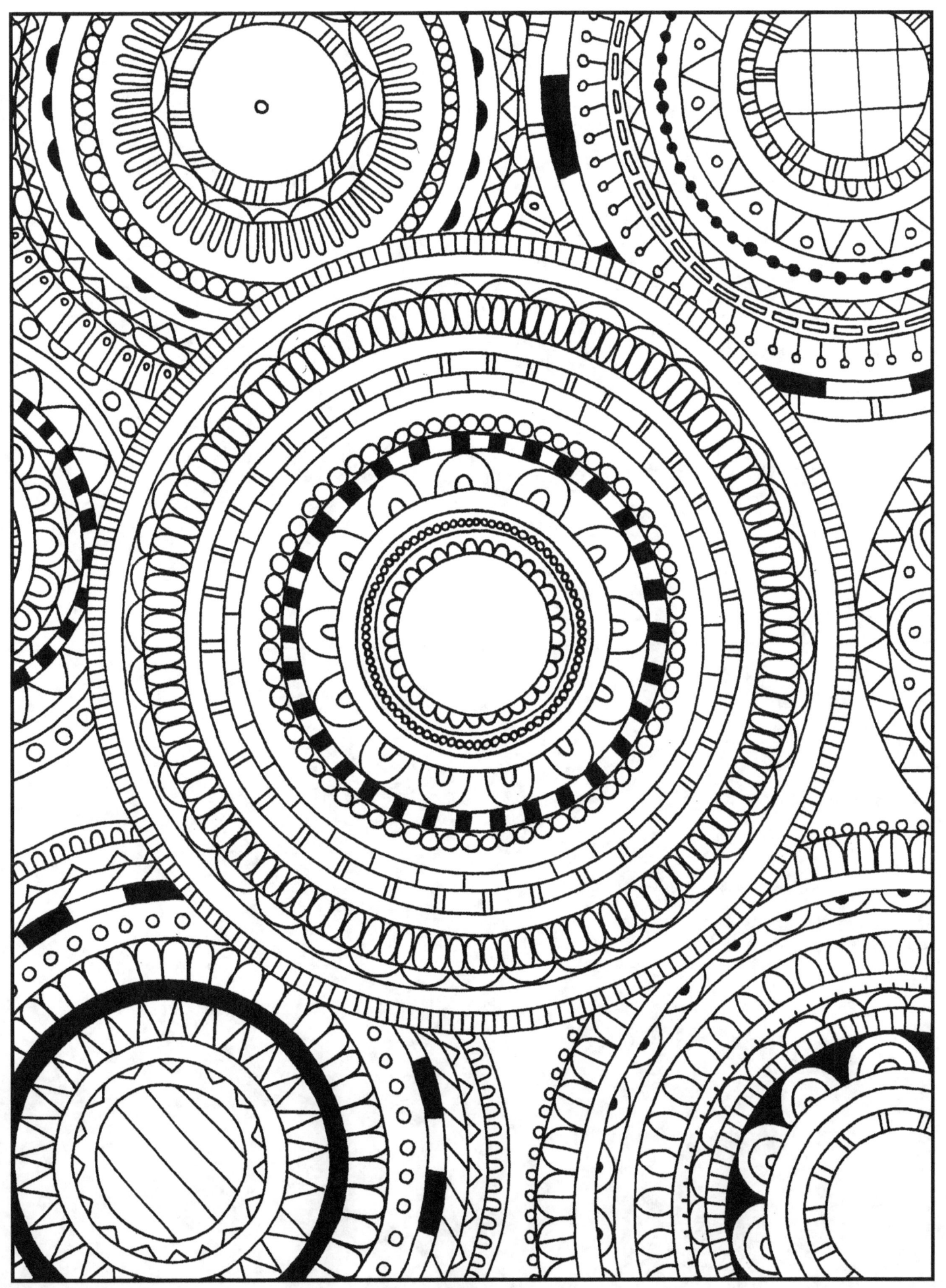

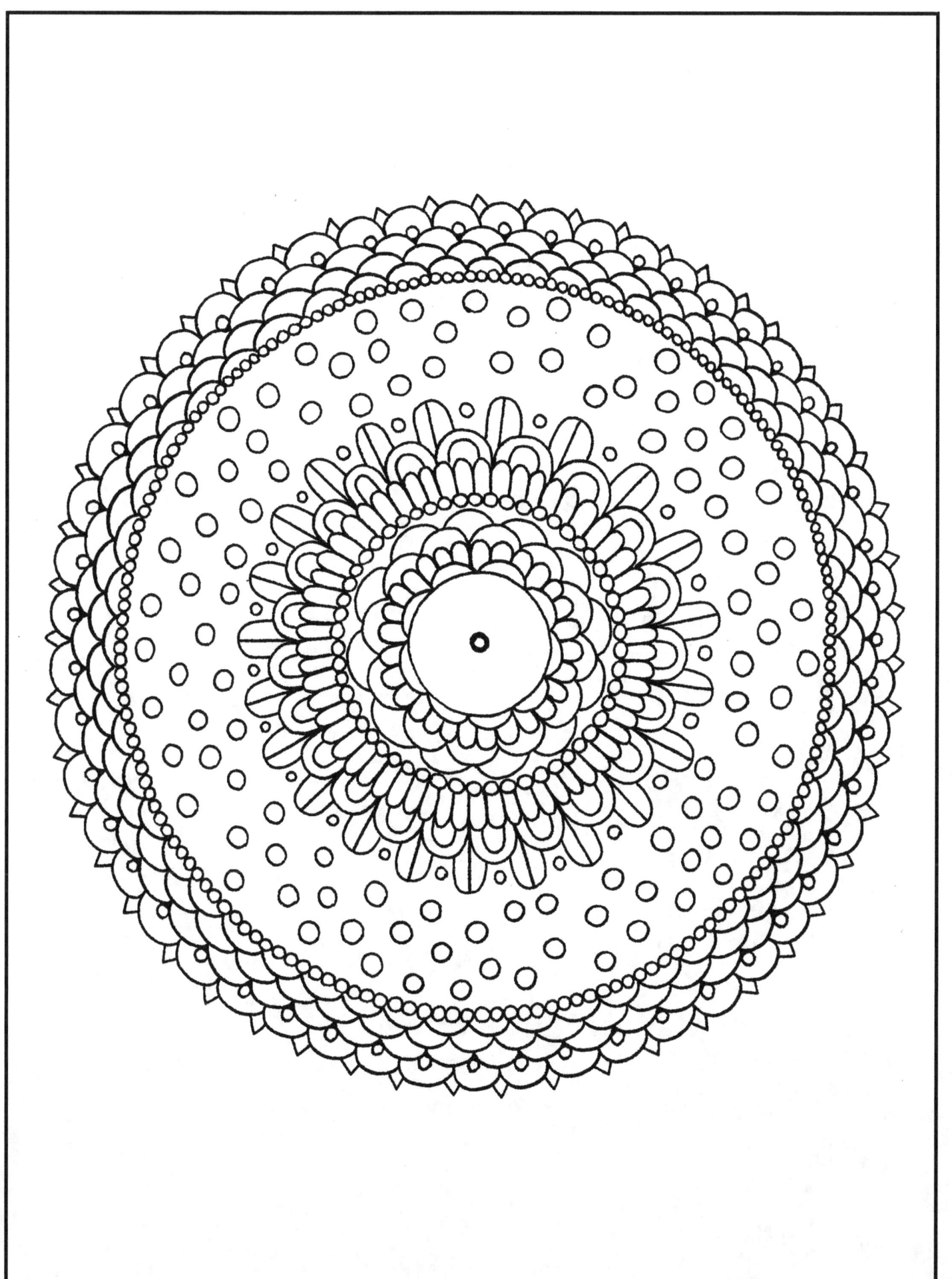

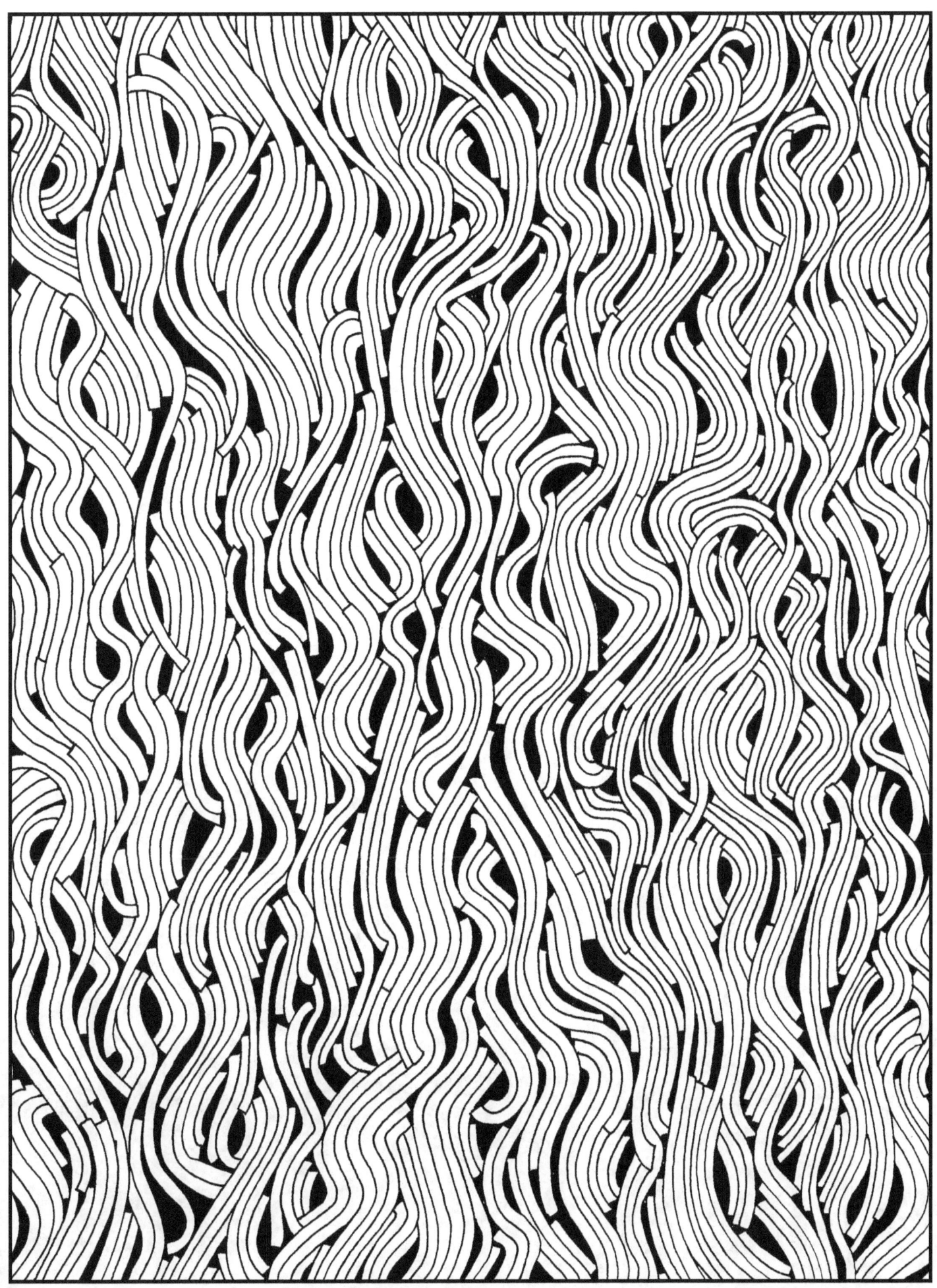

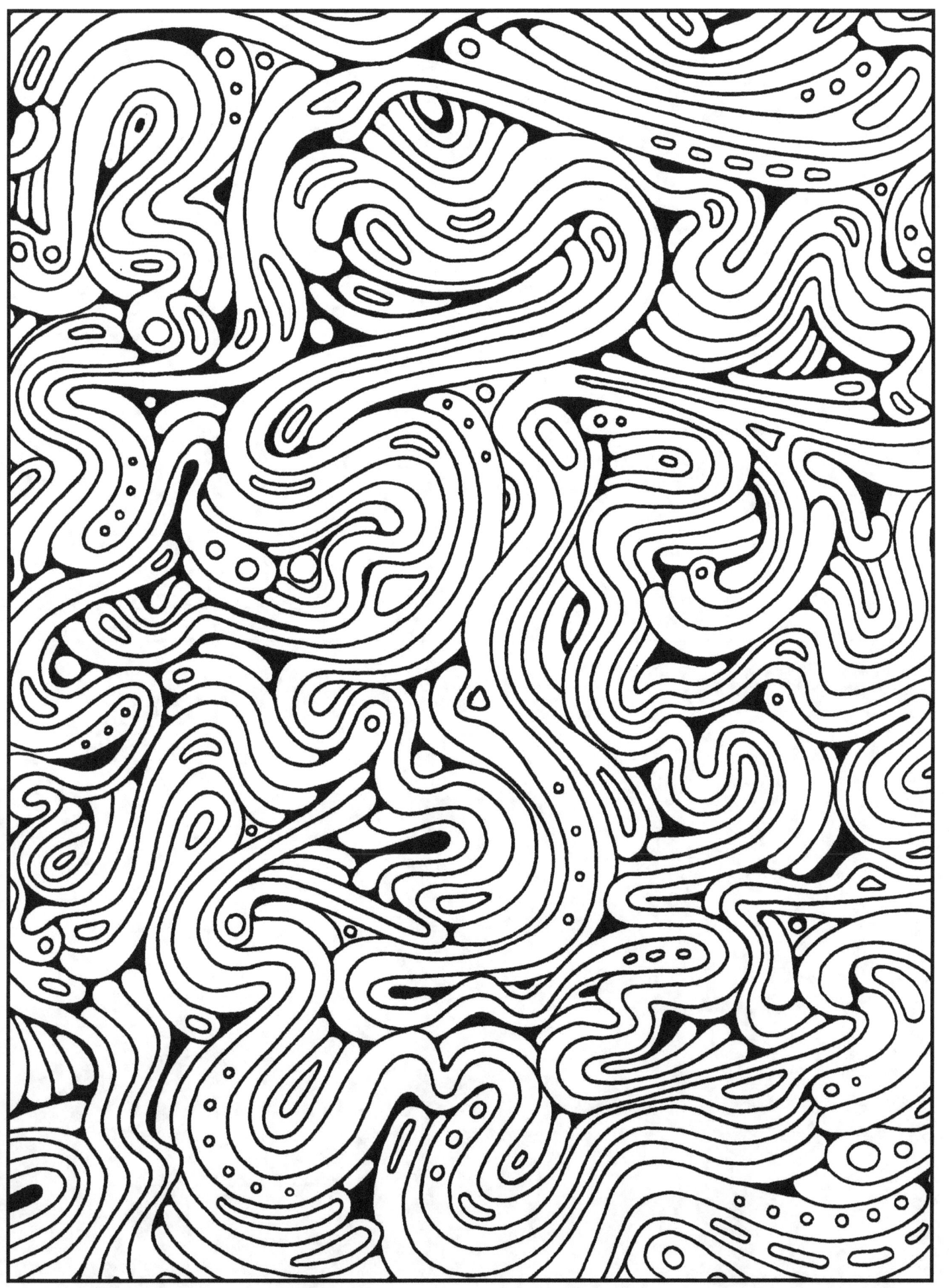